The VANISHING PROOFS *of* EVOLUTION

THOMAS F. HEINZE

CHICK
PUBLICATIONS

All Scripture quotations in this book are taken from the King James Version of the Bible.

Outside the USA:
Contact us to find a distributor near you, or see a list at **www.chick.com.**

Copyright © 2005 by Thomas F. Heinze

Published by:
CHICK PUBLICATIONS
P. O. Box 3500, Ontario, CA 91761-1019 USA
Tel: (909) 987-0771 • Fax: (909) 941-8128
www.chick.com
E Mail: postmaster@chick.com

Printed in the United States of America

ISBN: 978-0-7589-0570-3

Table of Contents

Table of Contents

Introduction

The Pillars of Evolution

The Theory of Evolution can be compared to a bridge erected on a number of seemingly sturdy pillars. Each pillar is assumed to be some solid scientific evidence inspiring faith in the whole system. Most people who believe in evolution were convinced by a limited amount of evidence; a number of classic "proofs" that have been used for years in books promoting the theory. These pillars sounded so scientific and compelling, multitudes put their faith in the bridge and walked out onto it. As the years passed, mighty floods of new evidence have swept these pillars away! The shaky old bridge still stands as a philosophic or religious belief system held in place by faith, tradition, and changing new arguments. The seemingly unanswerable "scientific proofs" which once gave the theory of evolution its credibility have been disproved by subsequent discoveries. This may or may not disprove the theory of evolution, but it does show that many of the most convincing arguments for it, probably including those that convinced you and will convince your children, are just not true.

Climbing Mount Improbable

I often use the term "uphill evolution" to describe the supposed upward progression from a primitive one-celled organism to all the complex living things around us. Dawkins, the famous atheist, has referred to it as "Climbing Mount Improbable."[1]

Evolutionists insist they don't claim that evolution is always moving upward, but in any direction. But any theory of evolution that does not also climb Mt. Improbable is an emasculated evolution that can never change bacteria into men and elephants. Downhill evolution can't start with a one-celled animal and make legs and eyes and brains. No combination of downhill or horizontal changes could ever transform the offspring of bacteria into anything but different bacteria. But, strange as it may seem, the typical examples used to convince students of evolution show downhill and horizontal changes rather than uphill. For example:

• Some fish in dark caves have lost their ability to see. They are often used to convince students, both of evolution in general, and that eyes evolved from spots on the skin.

• Sheep born with short, defective legs are another downhill example used to convince people that uphill evolution happens.

Evolutionists use only downhill and horizontal examples because evidence of uphill evolution is lacking. We will see why in chapter four.

We can all agree that if the available food changes, finches whose beaks are not strong enough to handle the

1   R. Dawkins, *Climbing Mount Improbable*, mentioned by Kevin L. Anderson, "Yeast Fails to Rise to Evolutionists' Expectations," *Creation Matters*, Jan./Feb., p. 1, 2002.

new food may die off, leaving alive the birds with stronger beaks. This is horizontal evolution. It does not show that finches evolved from dinosaurs, or became eagles, only that finches can adapt to changing environments.

Evolutionists have used the supposed loss of two or three toes as evidence that horses evolved. Losing toes is a downhill example. It does not show that horses evolved from a more primitive animal or even how toes got there in the first place. Evolutionists believe that evolution is caused mostly by mutations, yet uphill mutations producing new and more complex organs have not been observed.

The Missing "Missing Links"

Darwin wrote that if existing plants and animals evolved gradually, the fossils should show the stages of change. They don't! As we will see later, Darwin called this one of the greatest problems with his theory. They show distinct animals that continued as they were from the oldest fossils until they went extinct. The missing links are really missing! If every plant and animal evolved from a one-celled ancestor, what would have happened? David DeWitt puts it this way:

> "Successful macro-evolution [uphill] requires the addition of NEW information and NEW genes that produce NEW proteins that are found in New organs and systems."[2]

I would add that new organs would often require

[2]David A. DeWitt, "Hox Hype: Has Macro-evolution been Proven?" *Creation Matters,* a CRS publication, Jan./Feb. 2002, p. 10.

coordinated changes: not just the new proteins that make an eye, for example, but new proteins for muscle, blood vessels, bones, nerves, etc. which must all work together if the new eye is to see. If uphill evolution had actually produced every one of the millions of types of plants and animals and all their organs, uphill evidence should abound. If it did, wouldn't textbooks present uphill evidence, instead of asking us to believe in uphill evolution on the basis of downhill and horizontal evidence?

Read on! You may find that you, too, were brought to faith in uphill evolution by downhill evidence, false statements, and speculation!

1

Peppered Moths; Best Evidence for Evolution?

Moths and butterflies have an amazing life cycle. They start life as an egg from which a caterpillar hatches, eats, grows, and then goes through the pupa (chrysalis) stage, often after spinning a cocoon. In this stage the caterpillar actually melts to liquid goo which is then transformed into a butterfly or moth with two compound eyes rather than the six simple eyes of the caterpillar, six legs instead of the original 16, etc. It has reproductive organs that caterpillars did not have, and wings which fill out, open and fly off into the sunset. The process is called metamorphosis. With no flying or navigation lessons, monarch butterflies can not only fly with their new wings, but use their new instruments to fly thousands of miles to the spot, sometimes to the very tree, in California or Mexico where their ancestors spent the last winter.

Evolutionists claim that all animals evolved from a primitive one-celled creature as natural selection worked on mutations: errors in copying the DNA to pass it on to the next generation.

Which evolved first, a complex flying moth, or a relatively simpler caterpillar with no wings or reproductive organs? Neither! When Mrs. Moth lays an egg, its DNA already contains the directions that make the caterpillar, and then the pupa stage in which its organs melt into a liquid, and then the moth. Try to find a selective advantage that would make natural selection choose melting into liquid over being a caterpillar! There is none. All the information is already present in the DNA to direct the process from egg to caterpillar to liquid goo to butterfly or moth. To my knowledge, no reasonable way has ever been discovered, or even dreamed of, by which mutations could modify DNA, to produce the complex programs for all four of the moth's greatly differing but perfectly coordinated stages: egg, caterpillar, pupa, and moth.

The Best Evidence?

Despite having no idea how a moth could have evolved, almost every textbook promoting evolution from the 1960s on has used the peppered moth as the prize evidence to back up its teaching that evolution happens. You probably remember the pictures of light and dark peppered moths resting on light and dark tree trunks. (See Figure 1.) Before the industrial revolution, almost all the peppered moths in England had a generally light colored mixture of light and dark scales on their wings. At rest, they looked very similar to the white lichens which covered many tree trunks. Then, with the coming of the industrial revolution, the lichens died and the tree trunks became dark with the

Richard C. Lewontin, *Adaptation*, Scientific American, Sept. 1978, pg. 212.

Figure 1

smoke of industry. This robbed light colored moths of their protective coloration. Textbooks claim that birds then saw them resting on the trunks and ate them. Before long the majority of moths were dark.

Despite how scientific textbooks make this "proof" of evolution appear, the experiments behind the statements have come under attack. A recent book explains:

> "They were, and still are, hailed as 'Darwin's missing evidence' …'evolution in action.' Yet the history of the peppered moth has lately become a battlefield, the controversy becoming more inflamed by the moment."[1]

Why all this interest in a study of moths? In the early 20th century, Darwin's theory began to spread widely. However, evolutionists were becoming desperate. It was increasingly obvious that no scientific evidence was being found to support the theory. Perhaps this change in the peppered moth population might be the proof needed to confirm Darwin's theory.

Bernard Kettlewell, a medical doctor, and a moth and butterfly expert, studied the peppered moth. He became convinced that the darker peppered moths were becoming more numerous because their camouflage was better on the smoke-darkened tree trunks. He set up his experiments to show just that. Hooper writes that Kettlewell's moths:

> "…became the most celebrated experiment ever in evolutionary biology. By the 1960s the moths had conquered all the textbooks, influencing the minds of four decades of biology students. It is the slam dunk

[1]Judith Hooper, *Of Moths and Men: an Evolutionary Tail,* 2002, p. XV.

of natural selection, the paradigmatic story that converts high school and college students to Darwinism, the thundering left hook to the jaw of creationism."[2]

Before the moths' left hook thundered, other exceptionally powerful evidences for evolution had come smashing into the jaw of creationism. For 40 years Piltdown man skillfully beat up creationists until 1953 when it was discovered that this famous ape man was a deliberate hoax: a recent ape's jaw had been tinted and paired to an older human skull! After Piltdown had been beating up creationists for 40 years, someone noticed that his teeth still showed the marks of the file that had been used to make the lower teeth fit better with the uppers. Embarrassed evolutionists abandoned the Piltdown hoax.

A series of horse fossils then became the most powerful proof of evolution. These fossils were claimed to show the stages through which an animal with three and four toes passed as its foot became more and more simple (not more complex) gradually evolving into a modern horse with one toe on each foot. This left hook to creationism gradually lost its punch as more and more fossils were discovered. These creatures had not lived one after another in a neat evolutionary progression after all. They had galloped through the forest together.

Craig Holdrege, an American biology teacher who used the moth experiments to teach his students, was reading something by an English peppered moth researcher and friend of Kettlewell when he was struck by these words:

---

[2]Judith Hooper, *Of Moths and Men: an Evolutionary Tail,* 2002, p. XVii.

"In 25 years we have found only two betularia [peppered moths] on the tree trunk…"[3]

Kettlewell's whole proof of moth evolution depended on the moths resting on tree trunks where birds would see and eat them. Holdrege realized that what he had taught for years was not true. Under natural conditions peppered moths almost never rested on tree trunks! In fact, peppered moths are active at night, but spend their days on the lower side of branches in the shade of trees.[4]

The pictures of moths on tree trunks in textbooks are of two kinds. For the first pictures Kettlewell placed living moths on tree trunks.[5] Later pictures show dead moths stuck to the trunks.[6] Hooper says,

"By the early 90s, if not before, it was known to a small circle of scientists that what every textbook in the Darwinian universe said about industrial melanism was untrue."[7]

"Industrial melanism" is used here to refer to natural selection favoring dark moths after industry had smoked up the environment.

Most scientists, however, had no idea there were problems. Jerry Coyne, a University of Chicago Professor, learned when he read Michael Majerus's 1998 book, *Melanism: Evolution in Action*. When Coyne realized that what he had been teaching for years was at least partly

[3]Ibid., p. XViii.
[4]Ibid., pp. 260, 262, 265-266.
[5]Ibid., pp. 172:5-6, 264.
[6]Ibid., pp. 172:16-17, 264.
[7]Hooper, p. 265.

faked, he was "horrified." He wrote in his review of Majerus's book for the journal *Nature*:

> "My own reaction resembles the dismay attending my discovery, at the age of six, that it was my father and not Santa who brought the presents at Christmas eve."[8]

With the increased scrutiny, evolutionists have found many other problems with "the most celebrated experiment ever in evolutionary biology." Here are a few:

• For his famous experiment, Kettlewell brought in dark and light moths early in the mornings and put them on tree trunks where they do not normally rest, to see whether the birds would eat more dark or light moths. Since moths normally move around at night, if released then, they would have moved to their normal positions in the branches where neither Kettlewell nor the birds would be apt to find them. During the day, moths stay where they are put.[9]

• The experiment was based on the assumption that natural selection favored dark moths due to birds seeing lighter colored moths on tree trunks and eating them. This assumption was not accurate, both because moths don't normally rest on tree trunks and because birds seem not to eat many of them.[10]

• The findings were artificial. Setting out large numbers of moths on a few tree trunks taught birds to come there to

---

[8]Jerry Coyne, "Not Black and White," a review of Michael Majerus's *Melanism: Evolution in Action, Nature* 396, 1998, pp. 35-36, reported in Jonathan Wells, *Icons of Evolution, Science or Myth?* 2002, p. 157. See also Hooper pp. 283-286.

[9]Hooper, pp.110, 114, 260.

[10]Hooper, pp. 218, 265.

find food. Because of the unusual concentrations of moths put in unnatural and particularly obvious places, one critic called the experiment a study of "unnatural selection."[11]

• Some of the birds Kettlewell listed as eating his moths seem not to eat them at all under natural circumstances.[12]

• When Kettlewell did not get the results he wanted, he changed the design of his experiments until he did.[13]

• Both diet and temperature have also been found to cause dark forms of the moths to be produced. Perhaps the gene for dark moths is always present, but is sometimes turned off.[14]

• Hooper writes that this is not one of those experiments that has been verified by lots of other scientists. She quotes one who tried and said:

> "It doesn't happen… David West tried it. Cyril Clark tried it. I tried it. Everybody tried it. No one gets it."[15]

Once people understand that this famous experiment does not show what it is claimed to show, they generally take one of two attitudes. Michael Majerus wrote the book that first exposed the problems and the false science. He says it teaches kids to believe in natural selection, which is true, so we should still use it even though the experiment itself was false.

The other attitude is seen in Jerry Coyne, who wrote the

[11] Hooper, p. 267.
[12] Hooper, pp. 243, 258.
[13] Hooper, pp. 256-257, 292.
[14] Hooper, pp. 280-282, 287.
[15] Hooper, p. 296, quoting Professor Bruce Grant of the College of William and Mary in Virginia. See also p. 272.

review of Majerus's book. He was horrified to find that he had been conned into teaching something false. Because he desires honesty in science and science books, he refused to continue teaching the contrived evidence.

What will the school books do? At the moment, this "proof of evolution" is still the standard textbook evidence that evolution is taking place,[16] but the two most recent textbooks I have checked don't have it.

"Uphill Evolution" a Myth

An even greater problem is the fact that this most convincing argument for evolution has never shown any uphill evolution, but only horizontal. Dark peppered moths are not more highly evolved than light peppered moths, and peppered moths never became anything other than peppered moths. None ever became bats or humming birds, or even a different kind of moth. Only the color changed. What's more, when ecological awareness later led to the cleaning up of the industrial smoke, many of the trees returned to their former light color, and so did the moths!

Whether or not future textbook authors will use the peppered moth argument, when I was in school many considered it "the story that converts high school and college students to Darwinism, the thundering left hook to the jaw of creationism."[17]

---

[16]Prentice Hall, *Biology, the Living Science,* 1998, p. 233; Adison-Wesley, *Biology,* 2nd Edition, p. 251; and most biology textbooks.
[17]Hooper, p. XVii.

If you believe in evolution, some of what convinced you was probably the story that birds picked peppered moths off tree trunks.

To impress on us the influence the moth story has had, Hooper named her last chapter, "A Damn Good Story." Sure, it was a really convincing story, and that is what she meant, but it is also a damning story. Jesus Christ said:

> "I am the way, the truth, and the life: no man cometh unto the Father, but by me." (John 14:6)

Many have not come to the Father through Jesus Christ because their schoolbooks have convinced them to believe in the way of evolution, a way that has led many into doubt, skepticism and atheism. No one comes to the Father except by Jesus Christ. We have that on the authority of Jesus, who is the truth.

If peppered moths helped build your faith in Darwinism, your faith is partially founded on evidence you now know was faulty. Not all the evidence was false, but even what was true was not uphill. The peppered moth is an example of horizontal evolution. It only shows that peppered moths can come in more than one color.

2

Does an Embryo Relive Its Evolution?

Ernest Haeckel, a follower of Darwin, believed that at the beginning of a new life, as the embryo grows, it passes through the various stages of its evolutionary history. He called this idea the biogenetic law, and popularized it in 1866 with a series of pen and ink drawings which is still used to convince students of evolution.

Faked Drawings

Haeckel drew the embryos as he felt they should have looked if each embryo passed through the same stages in its development that its evolutionary ancestors had followed in the course of their evolution. These drawings were then presented as evidence that an embryo actually goes through the same stages its species had gone through while evolving to its present state. Its best known claim is that at one stage of development a human embryo looks like a fish with gills. This stage is supposed to show that humans evolved from fish, and that as the human embryo

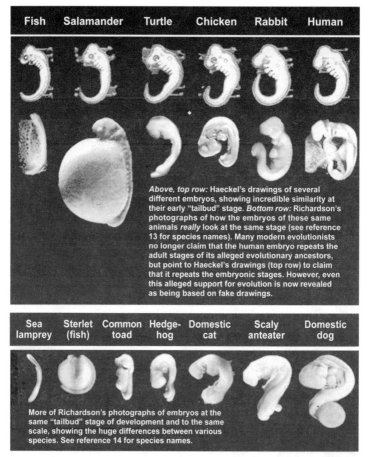

Fish	Salamander	Turtle	Chicken	Rabbit	Human

Above, top row: Haeckel's drawings of several different embryos, showing incredible similarity at their early "tailbud" stage. *Bottom row:* Richardson's photographs of how the embryos of these same animals *really* look at the same stage (see reference 13 for species names). Many modern evolutionists no longer claim that the human embryo repeats the adult stages of its alleged evolutionary ancestors, but point to Haeckel's drawings (top row) to claim that it repeats the embryonic stages. However, even this alleged support for evolution is now revealed as being based on fake drawings.

Sea lamprey	Sterlet (fish)	Common toad	Hedge-hog	Domestic cat	Scaly anteater	Domestic dog

More of Richardson's photographs of embryos at the same "tailbud" stage of development and to the same scale, showing the huge differences between various species. See reference 14 for species names.

Figure 2 Photos kindly supplied by Dr. Michael K. Richardson. They originally appeared in M.K. Richardson et al., "There Is No Highly Conserved Embryonic Stage in the Vertebrates: Implications for Current Theories of Evolution and Development," *Anatomy and Embryology* 196(2):91-106, 1997 ©Springer-Verlag GmhH & Co., Tiergartenstrasse, 69121, Heidelberg German. Reproduced with permission.

grows, each human passes again through that stage.

The drawings were exposed as fraudulent by a number of scientists as early as 1874, while Haeckel was still alive. Despite being exposed, Haeckel's theory is often presented as a law of science. Some of his drawings are still in schoolbooks today.

Jonathan Wells, in *Icons of Evolution*, critiques seven biology textbooks, mostly from 1998 and 1999, which use Haeckel's drawings.[1] In spite of Haeckel's drawings being exposed as fakes, many, even among today's leading evolutionists, still think they are true. Wells writes,

> "In February 2000 textbook-writer Douglas Futuyma posted a message to a Kansas City internet forum in response to a creationist who had accused him of lying by using Haeckel's embryos in his 1998 textbook [advanced college level], *Evolutionary Biology.* In his defense Futuyma explained that before reading the critic's accusation he had been unaware of the discrepancies between Haeckel's drawings and the actual vertebrate embryos."

Futuyma, though a well-known, well-informed, and highly respected evolutionist, probably never would have learned about the hoax had that creationist not told him in the email.

A few honest evolutionists continue to discover the hoax, and expose it. For example, M. K. Richardson discovered the hoax and in 1998 exposed it in the journal *Science,* saying:

[1]pp.102-107; as an example see Prentice Hall *Biology, The Living Science,* 1998, p. 223.

"Haeckel's drawings of 1874 are substantially fabricated. In support of this view, I note that his oldest 'fish' image is made up of bits and pieces from different animals —some of them mythical. It is not unreasonable to characterize this as 'faking.' Later editions of Haeckel's drawings were somewhat more accurate... Sadly, it is the discredited 1874 drawings that are used in so many British and American biology textbooks today."[2]

Richardson's article in *Science* stirred up letters to the editor insisting that since the embryo evidence is in so many textbooks, it must be true. I followed the discussion as Richardson answered the objections with more letters published in *Science*. The few people who read that journal seemed to eventually be convinced because the letters objecting to Richardson's article stopped. Now things will probably continue as they were until another scientist discovers the fraud, becomes embarrassed at having been deceived, and writes an article in another journal. At this writing the fraud has been making converts to evolution for almost 150 years. It makes one wonder, would the textbooks still use this fake evidence to convince people of evolution if there was real evidence they could use instead?

To avoid criticism, some schoolbooks show short, hard to identify portions of Haeckel's drawings, and others attribute them to someone else. In these cases, old fraud is hidden by new fraud, and Haeckel continues to make converts to evolution.

[2]Michael K. Richardson, *Science*, Vol. 281, 28 Aug. 1998.

What makes the idea believable is that there really are some similarities between a human embryo and some lower forms of life. Most animals are somewhat similar in basic structure, being made of cells, and also in basic function, needing nutriment, oxygen, and a way to dispose of waste materials. The drawings were faked, however, by adding similarities that don't really exist in order to claim that the embryo passes through one after another of the stages of its evolutionary history.

The resemblances to lower animals that really do exist are usually quite superficial. In the case of the famous "gill slits," the embryo, when a month old, has certain folds on what is becoming its neck, but these folds never have either the function or the material of gills. The tissue of the folds is actually developing into jaw, neck, etc., not into gills, yet some young people are still told that their embryos went through a gilled stage, and are fed the conclusion: "...fish and humans shared an ancient gilled ancestor."[3] Or just that men evolved from fish.

While I was writing this book it was posted on creationism.org. I expected to receive indignant emails from evolutionists when they found out they had been deceived; that their schoolbooks had hoodwinked them. I was not prepared, however, for who they would be indignant with. It was not with Haeckel who had perpetrated the scam. It was not even with the schoolbooks that promoted a known fraud for 150 years. On the contrary, they defended both Haeckel and the schoolbooks,

[3]John H. Postlethwait, Janet L. Hopson, McGraw-Hill, *The Nature of Life*, 1995, p. 373.

and were outraged with me! I was trying to rob them of an argument that for years has been effective in making converts for what seems to have become their religion. That, as far as I can tell, was more important than truth. If you feel this way too, don't think by writing me an indignant letter you can change my mind. Remember, the converts the faked embryos are bringing into your religion are taken from mine!

After our schools squeezed out the Creator, it was only natural for them to cleanse the schools of the Creator's 10 commandments as well. People, however, must believe something. Perhaps it is significant that one of the kids who ushered in the era of the schoolhouse shootings wore a tee shirt emblazoned with the words "survival of the fittest." Acting out that message by murdering his schoolmates is still not acceptable, but wearing the message seems not to have received any official criticism. The right to free speech extends to every one —except the Creator! A public school my own children attended would not even permit the use of the word Christmas because it is made up of two words, one of which is Christ.

Abortion

Back to Haeckel: Even though his theory was known to be false, teaching it as if it were true has influenced society in another way as well. I believe that some of your friends are having abortions today because Haeckel falsified his drawings in 1866. If you think this is far fetched, I still receive emails like the following:

"I furthermore don't believe that people are having

abortions due to his drawings which I acknowledge were not correct, however they weren't that far off, at conception you are not a human you are a group of cells, you do not become a human until you develop the traits of a human. By your reasoning, any cluster of developing cells is a human which obviously is not true."

As you see by this email, even after people acknowledge that Haeckel's arguments were not correct, some still find it hard to let go of the error.

In Oregon, where I live, not only abortion, but even murder of unborn babies has been legal. Read this quote from an article entitle "Fetus Stabbed In The Womb Dies," in the Portland newspaper, *The Oregonian*:

"The fetus of a woman who was stabbed in the abdomen two weeks ago by a man who came into her family's store died last week, police said. ...The woman continues to recover from her injuries at OHSU Hospital.

Clackamas County prosecutor Michael Regan said the death of the fetus is not expected to have legal implications for Alfredo Cortes-Villa, 20, of Salem, who has been charged with the attack. A fetus cannot be a homicide victim, according to state law. A homicide victim is defined as a human being who has been born and was alive at the time of the criminal act that led to his death."[4]

In the eyes of the law, the attacker did not kill an unborn baby, but just a fetus, and that was okay. Haeckel's

[4]Noelle Crombie, *The Portland Oregonian,* December 30, 2003.

drawings trumped a woman's right to choose. The legislators who wrote that law believed their biology textbooks which showed that at one stage an unborn baby looks much more like a fish or a pollywog than a human. Such power to convince is the reason the false drawings have been used so long.

Today, however, a powerful new influence is pulling society back toward truth. Ultrasound is showing an ever-growing number of people what their unborn babies really look like, and it is not like the drawings. It has taken 150 years, but the textbook position is becoming such an embarrassment that evolutionists may, with a sigh of reluctance, drop it.

Before I finished this book, a new national law burst onto the scene, making it illegal to stab unborn babies. *The Oregonian* includes this comment:

> "Opponents of the proposal, while saying they sympathized with the desire to severely punish anyone who would attack a pregnant woman, said they were troubled by the definition of the 'child in utero' covered under the bill as 'a member of the species Homo sapiens at any stage of development, who is carried in the womb."

The next paragraph adds these important words:

> "...they thought that once the definition was written into federal law, it would ultimately be used as an argument to overturn existing laws protecting abortion rights.'"[5]

[5] *The Oregonian*, March 26, 2004, p. A7.

I can understand why people who were convinced in school that the fetus goes through fish, pollywog and whatnot stages would be concerned about the new definition.

Let me clarify my position. I do not claim that a new embryo starts out as a perfect miniature adult. It starts out as two cells which unite and become one, and then grow from there. But a human baby is human from the moment of conception. The development of the embryo is directed by human DNA. There is no stage when the development of the embryo is determined by monkey DNA or fish DNA. The DNA for each form of life contains the instructions for constructing and maintaining its body. The instructions are written in a chemical code which is passed on to its offspring. RNA copies sections of the code as needed and takes them to the parts of the cell that translate and use the information. A baby fish is fish at every stage, just as a human baby is fully human even when it is not fully developed. It does not begin as a lower animal, and gradually become a human. You will never hear of a paternity test like this: "We tested the DNA of Megan's fetus and found that the father was a fish!"

3

Comparative Anatomy

You look like an ape! Though this is not completely true, but there are some real similarities. You both have two arms, two legs, and one head, though obviously there are also many differences. Because of the resemblances, evolutionists usually say that either man evolved from an ape (Australopithecus is favored) or that both had a common ancestor.

I do not deny that similarities can indicate family relationships. You probably resemble your father. But similarities often have a completely different meaning. In front of me are a number of books. Among these, two are almost identical. The covers are the same. The paper is of the same type. Only their thickness and the words inside are different. One who knows nothing about books might conclude that the thick book evolved from the thin one. The real reason for the similarity, though, is that the publisher designed a particular style that he is using for the books in this series. Evolution is only one of several possible reasons for similarity. The fact that both originated in the mind of the same designer is frequently the real reason behind similar design. Similarity of design is not proof that there was no designer.

Remember this when evolutionists claim to know that all life evolved from a single first cell because all living things have the same DNA-based system. Many who claim this similarity of design is evidence that all life evolved from an original cell, later turn around and contradict themselves with statements that life was begun by RNA and DNA came later. Other evolutionists who know that neither RNA nor its nucleotide building blocks will form outside of already living things, claim that the first life must have been some other substance, much simpler than either DNA or RNA.

A person interested in the creation/evolution debate wrote that when he was a student, one of his professors gave each person in the class an assortment of nails, screws, bolts, and other small objects. He told them it would help them understand evolution if they would start with the simplest and put all the articles in an evolutionary order. He did it, and felt that it really had made him a better evolutionist. After he went home, he realized that every one of those items had been designed and then made in a factory. Not one had evolved! The fact that things can be put in order from simple to complex is usually not evidence for evolution. A common designer is a better explanation of similarities among living things.

Think for a moment of the ability to fly. Evolution

would be very unlikely to be able to impart this ability. It demands the simultaneous appearance of features in the brain, nerves, tendons, muscles, blood vessels, bones, etc., all coordinated to work together. Evolutionists generally say that natural selection gradually perfected each part, but natural selection could not do a thing toward perfecting a feather, a muscle, or a whatever for flight, until after all of them already worked, and were so well coordinated that the bird could fly.

What makes flight an even greater problem to evolution though, is that it has been found in widely varying forms of life:

- Insects
- Birds
- Dinosaurs
- Bats

Evolutionists say no creatures with wings evolved from any other winged creature, but each evolved from a completely different ancestor with no wings. If it did, why is there no evidence of this in fossils? The oldest fossil of a bat, insect, flying dinosaur or bird, is of a completely formed bat, insect, dinosaur and bird. Their similarities are best explained by admitting that all were designed by the same God.

Evolutionists ask us to believe that the similarities of birds to bats reveal no relationship whatsoever, while at the same time asking us to believe that the similarities between men and apes show that they evolved from a common ancestor.

principle source of new genetic instructions which, starting with a single cell, have produced different plants and animals, including the more advanced species. They also trust that mutations perfected by natural selection brought all the organs into being: hands, gills, brains, etc. that a first cell did not have but that now exist. These mutations are random errors made in copying the cell's DNA instructions while passing them on to the next generation. Their frequency is increased by radiation, and other kinds of damage.

Mutations Usually "Downhill"

Thousands of diseases are known to be caused by mutations. These, however, are downhill mutations. No mutations have been identified which add complexity, or new genes containing new commands which could work together to produce the first head, or tail, or hand, or other body part that never existed before. The chance of accidental mutations making complex improvements in living things is about the same as that of an author's cat writing new and better chapters for his book by walking on his keyboard. You don't believe that aimless unplanned random happenings build better books, or that a traffic accident invented the wheel. Why believe random mutations produced your brain, or even your little toe?

Except for some mutations which are neutral, almost all are harmful. The *Encyclopedia Britannica* makes it clear:

> "Most mutations, however, turn out to be deleterious and often lead to some impairment or to death of the organism. To illustrate, it is unlikely that one can improve the functioning of a finely crafted watch by

dropping it from a tall building. The watch may run better, but this is highly improbable. Organisms are so much more finely crafted than the finest watch that any random change is even more likely to be deleterious."[1]

Ample evidence supports the encyclopedia's statement. Random errors in copying DNA really do produce defects —downhill evolution. Uphill evolution, the kind claimed to start with a simple one-celled creature and develop monkeys and redwood trees, is not based on evidence, but on faith in evolution. If any uphill mutations that increase biological complexity happen, no one can cite an example. Those who disagree usually use the example of sickle cell anemia, an often-lethal hereditary disease among humans which distorts the shape of the red blood cells. The distorted cells don't carry oxygen as well, but the genes that distort the red blood cells give some resistance to malaria, and this resistance is the most common illustration evolutionists give of a "helpful" mutation. While the mutation does have a helpful side effect, is it really a helpful mutation? Even if you think it is, it is not an uphill mutation. Mutations which distort the shape of red blood cells, and make them less efficient at doing their job of carrying oxygen are not causing uphill evolution. If uphill mutations exist, they are overwhelmingly outnumbered by harmful mutations, as the *The Britannica* so beautifully states.

Here is an experiment you can do yourself. Radiation

[1]"Life," *Encyclopedia Britannica*, 2002.

speeds up the mutation rate, so buy a trunk full of atomic waste and keep it under your bed. Maybe the children you have will be super evolved geniuses. Don't count on it!

The Fruit Fly Experiments

Many laboratory experiments were conducted to learn about the effect of mutations on evolution by studying the fruit fly. Since scientists could choose the mutations they wanted to preserve, many hoped to see good mutations gradually lifting the fruit flies to a higher level, developing new organs, and doing other things evolution is claimed to do.

The mutations studied caused a wide range of defects. While evolutionists believe many constructive mutations also occur, they have been difficult to pin down. People who disagree usually tell me about the mutation that repeated the genes for wings on a fruitfly, adding an extra pair. They hung down and got in the way, and did not function, so would be eliminated by natural selection.

The useless wings do help us understand what is involved in adding new organs. For mutations to write the code for wings, if they had not existed before, would have required coding for many new proteins for muscles, nerves, blood supply, etc. which would all work together. To duplicate wings that already existed and worked would only require duplication of the genes for the whole package. You can get about the same amount of totally new information by making photocopies of already existing pages of text. In the fruitfly example, however, the genes for other body parts that should have worked with the new wings were not duplicated, so the wings did not work. The observed mutations of fruit flies were not steps toward their becoming men, birds, or even butterflies. They did not add new information that would make novel new organs. They did not even duplicate enough of the already existing wing genes so the added wings could function. The famous French zoologist Pierre Grassé wrote:

> "The fruitfly (Drosophila melanogaster), the favorite pet insect of the geneticists, whose geographical, biotopical, urban and rural genotypes are now known inside out, seems not to have changed since the remotest times."[2]

Since fruit fly experiments did not give the desired result, E. coli bacteria began to be used. Bacteria have new generations much more rapidly than the flies. The results? According to Grassé,

> "The reader will agree that it is surprising, to say the least, to want to prove evolution and to discover its mechanisms and then to choose as a material for this study a being which practically stabilized a billion years ago!"[3]

More recent evolutionists tell us the situation is even worse and refer to the oldest fossils which they say "are from rocks about 3.55 billion years of age, and they look identical to bacteria still on Earth today."[4] Many of today's evolutionists believe the bacteria were "practically stabilized" not just a billion years ago, but 3.55 billion years ago.

[2]*Evolution of Living Organisms,* 1977, p. 130.
[3]*Ibid.,*1977 p. 87.
[4]Peter D. Ward, Donald Brownlee, *Rare Earth, Why Complex Life is Uncommon in the Universe,* 2000, p. 57.

Bacteria, which often split off another generation every 15 minutes, evolve very rapidly in theory. They are designed to adapt well to changing environments, but their mutations are not producing fish or worms, or arms or wings, just more bacteria, evidently no more advanced than those claimed to have lived 3.55 billion years ago.

David DeWitt describes what would be required if the theory of evolution were true:

"Successful macro-evolution requires the addition of NEW information and NEW genes that produce NEW proteins that are found in New organs and systems."[5]

Recessive Mutations

Public school textbooks often downplay the proportion of harmful mutations or state: "Natural selection eliminates the harmful mutations." However, around two thirds of all mutations are recessive. That is, they only show up in the offspring which inherit the same mutation from both parents. Recessive mutations cannot be rapidly eliminated, because natural selection can only eliminate the diseased offspring, not the two thirds which carry the disease and pass it on, but are not affected themselves. This schoolbook quotation is right:

"Because natural selection operates only on genes that are expressed, it is very slow to eliminate harmful recessive mutations."[6]

---

[5]David A. DeWitt, "Hox Hype: Has Macro-evolution Been Proven?" *Creation Matters,* a CRS Publication, Jan./Feb. 2002, p. 10.
[6]Holt, Rinehart and Winston, *Modern Biology*, 2002, p. 304.

In addition, the same mutations tend to be repeated. Because of this and the difficulty of eliminating recessive mutations, some genetic diseases have become widespread.

Clusters of Mutations

To develop a new organ would require a number of mutations that would code for the new muscles, nerves, bones, etc. that would work in a coordinated way in the new organ. The various parts of a new organ would need to be produced at about the same time to start working together before any essential part could be eliminated. If mutations developed that coded for a few of the necessary parts, but not those which would have to work together with them, they would not be helpful. What good is a new bone without muscles to move it, with no blood supply or no nerves? Mutations that are not functional tend to be eliminated by natural selection.

Would a big cluster of mutations all at the same time solve the problem? Since most mutations are harmful, if an organism were to receive a cluster of mutations large enough to include a few helpful mutations that would work together, the cluster would also contain many more harmful mutations that cause genetic diseases. Natural selection eliminates harmful mutations by eliminating the whole organism which contains them, so organisms which receive clusters of mutations don't evolve, they die.

Point Mutations

Minimal mutations that command the change of only one amino acid in one protein are called *point mutations*. Because clusters of mutations tend to kill the organisms that receive them, point mutations are considered the most important to evolution. The individual that receives a point mutation often survives. Drake says:

> "...point mutations are likely to allow the afflicted individual to survive and reproduce, and may thus be transmitted and affect subsequent generations. In terms of human suffering, therefore, the summed effects of single gene mutations probably exceed the deleterious effects of changes in chromosome number or arrangement."[7]

Point mutations often survive, but each one only modifies one amino acid in one protein; not nearly enough to produce a new organ. Until a new organ is complete enough to be of some use to the individual it is in, it tends to be eliminated, so it is hard to see how point mutations could ever make new organs.

Once we understand that neither point mutations nor larger clusters of mutations can make new organs, we see why books promoting evolution use downhill and horizontal examples instead of uphill examples. If you are being taught that mutations have caused evolution, a not-too-threatening question to ask your teacher is: "Were new organs developed by point mutations, or larger clusters of mutations?" According to the answer, you can quote a paragraph or two from this book, and politely ask the teacher to explain it. Don't insist and flunk the course, just get some thinking started.

[7]John W. Drake, "Environmental Mutagenic Hazards," *Science*, Vol. 187, Feb. 14, 1985, p. 505.

5

Vestigial Organs, Evolution's Leftovers?

Evolutionists argue that organs exist which have no function, but were useful in less evolved animals. They call them rudimental or vestigial organs. In the search for proof of evolution, past generations of scientists found in humans around one hundred eighty organs with no known function. Some of these are more highly developed in lower animals.

These organs were once greatly used as evidence for evolution. However, with the progress of science, it was discovered that many of them were glands that produced very necessary hormones. Others were found to function in the embryonic stage, while some functioned only as a reserve when other organs were destroyed. Some functioned only in periods of emergency. Today, very few human organs are still claimed to be vestigial, and many scientists now believe all are functional. This seems strange to me because most mutations are harmful, and I would expect it to be easy for them to destroy organs. To form a new organ would seem very difficult. It would require random changes to write code for new proteins to form muscle, bone, nerves, blood vessels, all coordinated and working together. It would seem that a mutation which destroyed the functionality of any one of these parts of an organ could make the organ lose its function. I, like the evolutionists, would expect there to be many vestigial organs, and am surprised that, with the increase in knowledge, those considered vestigial have been so reduced.

Evolutionists who write to me about this claim there are still many vestigial organs. But they generally change the argument from organs in humans to those in some animal whose organs are as little known now as human organs were when this argument was first used.

Downhill Evolution

Since new organs cannot be shown to have been developed by evolution, the argument from vestigial organs is another attempt to use downhill evidence to prove uphill evolution. The loss of genetic information is not proof that evolution can generate new information to construct new organs. It is as if someone demonstrated that a kid with a hammer can ruin the hood of your new car, and used that as evidence that your car was built by a kid with a hammer. Evolutionists use downhill examples to convince us of uphill evolution because they don't have uphill examples.

The Appendix

The vestigial organ which has been most commonly used as a "proof of evolution" is the appendix.

In some "less evolved" animals the appendix is larger than that of man. It is stated that man evolved from hypothetical ancestors with larger, functioning appendixes, keeping his appendix but losing its functions. There are, however, animals considered less evolved that have smaller appendixes than man, and many animals have no appendixes at all.

According to the *Encyclopedia Britannica* at the time when this argument was still very popular,

> "Animals that have the same organ in a fully developed and functional condition are believed to be close to the ancestry of the animals having the vestigial organ."[1]

This idea would put man closer in ancestry to the marsupials and rabbits in which the appendix is well developed than to many monkeys which do not have them. When discussing vestigial organs, a typical modern schoolbook says:

> "The human appendix, a small fingerlike projection from the intestine, also has no known function."[2]

This statement is not true. It has been known for a number of years that man's appendix has a function. Like his tonsils, it contains lymphatic tissue which captures and fights infection. If it had no function, why would it not have been eliminated? Instead, it has a good blood supply, another evidence that it's function is valuable.[3]

---

[1] *Encyclopedia Britannica*, Vol. 1, 1967, p. 983.
[2] Holt, Rinehart and Winston, *Modern Biology*, 2002, p. 290.
[3] Ken Ham, Carl Wieland, "Your Appendix, It's There For a Reason," *Creation,* Dec.-Feb. 1997. Includes references to non creationist sources.

Scalp and Ear Muscles

The muscles that move the scalp and ears are often cited as vestigial in humans. Horses use them to shoo off flies. In humans they supposedly have lost their function, and become vestigial. Mine are not vestigial. I can easily move my scalp and ears and often twitch one or the other to chase off flies. Evolutionist writers who use this argument are seriously handicapped. They have to lift a hand from the keyboard for every fly that approaches, so I will probably eliminate them in the struggle for the survival of the fittest.

Where Did New Organs Come From?

Whether vestigial organs are many or few, they are another use of downhill examples to support uphill evolution. It is easy to see how random copying errors could ruin good organs. The real problem is: how could such mutations produce functional new organs? It is not only difficult in theory, but the fossil record is not much help. In addition, if the millions of organs present in living things were constantly developing in the past, why don't we see new organs developing today? People could probably benefit from radar, or sonar like the bats. We could communicate from farther away with radio waves or microwaves, and how about some really new organs based on ideas we have never heard of? The truth is that incomplete structures that don't function yet would be eliminated. They would not go on to become organs.

Random mutations can easily destroy functional organs, but how could they possibly create new genetic code that directs the construction and coordination of functional interconnecting parts?

If the appendix, and the muscles of the ear and scalp really had lost all function, they would be good evidence for downhill evolution. Genetic information would have been lost. The textbooks, however, don't cite these examples to convince students that mutations cause downhill evolution, but to help them believe in uphill evolution. Remember, bacteria cannot develop into biochemists by losing genetic information no matter how much they lose.

Be alert! Examine every "evidence" for evolution you are shown to see if it demonstrates a loss or gain in information. It's an eye opener! If evidence for the evolution of new organs exists, the textbooks would use it, instead of wasting time and space on organs they claim have lost their function?

New Animals and Endangered Species

The lack of evidence for uphill evolution is as true for new groups of animals as it is for new organs. The environmental movement is a direct result of the fact that evolution is not producing new types of animals and plants to replace the ones that die out. Environmentalists have a good reason to try to save the endangered species. When they become extinct, they are gone forever. If the theory of evolution were valid, who would care what became extinct? For each category of plants or animals that died out, several "superior" ones would spring up to take its place. In the real world, we are left with one less.

6

Uniformitarian Geology

Before Darwin, people generally believed that disasters, such as floods, particularly the great flood at the time of Noah, stirred up and redeposited much of the sediment that now forms the rocks of the earth's crust. In 1830 Sir Charles Lyell wrote *Principles of Geology,* opposing the flood and teaching uniformitarian geology. He denied not only the great flood, but all rapid geologic changes. He claimed that in the past, geologic processes like erosion and deposition of sediment occurred very slowly. Because there are some very thick deposits of sediments, this provided long ages that opened the way to the theory of evolution:

"...One of the most important influences of uniformitarianism was on the development of the theory of evolution. Charles Darwin obtained a copy of Lyell's *Principles of Geology* shortly before boarding the Beagle and read it on the voyage that led to his theory."[1]

[1] *Grolier Interactive Encyclopedia*, 1998, "Uniformitarianism"

Uniformitarianism, with its denial of all rapid change in order to get rid of really big floods, not only provided Darwin with the long ages evolution needed, but soon became the majority opinion among geologists. It maintained that position until the 1990s, though some geologists abandoned it earlier, and some still believe it.

One factor in the growing dissatisfaction with the exclusively slow geological processes of uniformitarianism was the growing acceptance of the evidence for the Missoula flood that had occurred during the ice age. A glacier had moved in and dammed up a river northeast of present day Missoula Montana. As the water accumulated behind the glacier, a huge lake was formed. Finally the water lifted the glacier and shoved it aside. From Montana, the flood rushed through eastern Oregon and Washington, and plunged toward the sea. Its power cut through rock as well as dirt, digging out much of the Columbia river gorge. The flood covered Portland with around 400 feet of water which had been traveling an estimated 60 to 80 miles an hour. As the flood hit the Willamette Valley, it spread out, causing the waters to move more slowly, and deposit 50 feet of top soil over much of the Willamette Valley before carrying the rest out to sea. At its height, the flood's water equaled around 10 times the output of all the world's rivers. Some think the blockage, lake building and flooding may have taken place more than once.

Evidence for the Missoula Flood was discovered and presented in 1917, but geologists were committed to uniformitarianism. They were afraid that accepting any big flood might give the Genesis flood a foot in the door, and they didn't know yet where all the water came from, so they ignored or denied the evidence. It was in the 1950s after a generation of geologists had gone to their graves that significant numbers of geologists began to accept the Missoula flood. By around 1968 so much evidence had built up, the flood became almost undeniable.

Other evidence against uniformitarianism was equally compelling. To support their idea of long periods of time, uniformitarianists, also called gradualists, would sometimes teach that dead plants or animals would lie on the ground or in oxygen free water on the bottom of the ocean for hundreds or thousands of years. They would be very gradually covered with sediment before starting to fossilize. Evolutionists badly needed a long time for their theory to seem plausible, but was this the way to get it? In the real world plants and animals that are fossilized are covered with sediment rapidly, usually by flood-born sediments or a mudslide. Bodies laying exposed for months or years are eaten or rot away. Leftover bones are spread around, and erode away. After a short time no trace is left. If they die in oxygen free water, their bodies are eaten by anaerobic bacteria.

For more than a hundred years the religious devotion of most geologists to an impossible theory, led them to ignore and explain away such things. As time passed, however, the evidence became inescapable. The geologic theory that did so much to bring in evolution was wrong! Geologists were unprepared, and had to grab a passing branch to break their fall. The evidence forced them to bail out of uniformitarianism before they had found a solid new position to jump to. They now call themselves actualists, or modified uniformitarianists, or old earth geologists. They accept the fact that some floods really have laid down in a few days quantities of sediments that uniformitarianists claimed took from thousands to many millions of years, but they still don't accept the Genesis flood! The disbelief in the Genesis flood is almost an article of faith, a core dogma that can't be abandoned by evolutionary geologists.

What then happened to all the time evolution needed? Geologists today are in the difficult position of admitting that most of the earth's sediments were built up much more rapidly than was admitted under uniformitarianism but they still believe in the same long ages. They now admit it did not take long to build up the layers of sediment, but still believe in the same long periods of time as the uniformitarianists. They now claim that, instead of the time passing while layers of sediments were being built up a grain at a time, most of the time passed between the layers: after one layer was laid down, and before the next. Uniformitarianists said the strata from the beginning of the Cambrian layer near the bottom of the Grand Canyon to the top, covered 555 million years. During that time, the sediment was for the most part being gradually laid down, a grain at a time.

Actualist geologists today admit that the sediments were laid down rapidly. After careful calculations one estimated to me the time it took to build up the sediments at 2.5 million years. Amazingly, however, he and the other old earth geologists accept the same 555 million years as the old gradualist uniformitarianists. To do it, they hide all but 2.5 million years of that time between the layers. They believe that several layers were laid down, then many years passed in which some layers may have been erased from the record. Then more layers were laid down, etc. They tuck a hundred million years between one layer and another, then ten million between two other layers, etc.

In some cases it is obvious that some time really did pass between layers. After a layer of sediment has been laid down, canyons begin to be carved out, so when another layer is laid down, the contact line is no longer flat. Yet, in some cases actualists claim that millions of years passed between layers that have a flat contact for miles and show little or no evidence that any time had passed.

Many first believed in evolution because they were taught in school that the earth's sediments were deposited so slowly that the time available to evolution was immense. Now you know some of the reasons why most geologists abandoned the old uniformitarianism, the foundation on which evolution was built. You now know that the foundation was not true, and that today's actualism is a compromise between the actual evidence and the false foundation that makes you free to consider other options.

7

Do Fossils Prove Evolution?

Darwin, like many today, thought natural selection caused each kind of plant or animal to gradually and constantly evolve into new kinds of plants or animals.

The Missing Links are Missing

Unlike many textbook writers today, Darwin admitted in writing that the fossil record did not show the constant change his theory predicted:

> "But just in proportion as this process of extermination has acted on an enormous scale, so must the number of intermediate varieties, which have formerly existed, be truly enormous. Why then is not every geological formation and every stratum full of such intermediate links? Geology assuredly does not reveal any such finely graduated organic chain; and this, perhaps, is the most obvious and serious objection which can be urged against the

theory. The explanation lies, as I believe, in the extreme imperfection of the geological record."[1]

The fossil record shows that many kinds of plants and animals have lived and then become extinct. Their earlier and later fossils show no significant difference. There is no evidence of the gradual evolution of one animal into another that Darwin's theory requires. He was right in admitting that fossils do not show one animal gradually changing into another. The intermediate links between one major category and another are lacking. The missing links are really missing. Darwin believed the transitional steps must really be there and would be found as more fossils were dug up. Since Darwin's time, many more fossils have been discovered, but fossils that show one kind of plant or animal becoming another are still missing.

In addition, fossils showing the development of organs are also absent. Take wings for an example. Flight is a complex process. Evolving it would take many tries over a long period of time, leaving behind fossils of unsuccessful tries with quarter wings, half wings, etc. They don't exist.

In addition, flying insects, birds, dinosaurs, and mammals are not claimed to have evolved from a first winged creature. Evolutionists claim instead that each group of flying creatures evolved from some animal in its own group that did not have wings. None of them left transitional fossils to show how wings developed. Fossils of wings and other organs show up in the fossil record completely formed.

[1] Charles Darwin, *The Origin of Species,* Chapter 10, First Collier Books Edition, p. 308.

Many biology books, instead of admitting the problem as Darwin did, present a make-believe fossil record which supports the evolutionist point of view, hoping the reader will believe it is real.

One evolutionist, after reading this book while I was writing it on www.creationism.org, wrote to object that the development of the human skull showed the smooth gradual evolution that I was denying. He referred me to a website that lined up skulls so you could clearly see that each skull on the way to becoming human was slightly larger than the one before. The first thing I noticed was that this website placed the skull of Neanderthal man just before that of modern man. It was just the right amount smaller than that of modern man to show the gradual evolution of modern man from Neanderthal. Since I knew the average Neanderthal brain was 10 to 20% larger than ours today, I immediately noticed the falsification. They had just photographically reduced the size of the Neanderthal skull to make it look smaller than ours to fake the smooth transition they were claiming to prove.

Eyes

My favorite answer, to those who claim that the transitional fossils exist, is in the Cambrian layer that for years was considered the very beginning of the fossil record. Because all 30 of the major categories called "phyla" which exist today appeared suddenly, fully formed, in the Cambrian, it is referred to as the Cambrian explosion.

Most of us have been taught that eyes gradually evolved

step by step from spots on the skin. What do the fossils show? Way down there among these very old Cambrian fossils was that of an animal called the trilobite that crawled along the bottom of the sea. It is one of the index fossils used to identify the Cambrian era. The fossils of its eyes are almost unbelievable to evolutionists. Here are two quotes from amazed evolutionists from a fascinating article on Trilobite eyes in *Reason and Revelation,* Apologetics Press, Oct. 03, along with their documentation of the quotes:

> "Paleontologist Niles Eldredge of the American Museum of Natural History commented:

> **'...We can be justifiably amazed that these trilobites, very early in the history of life on Earth, hit upon the best possible lens design that optical physics has ever been able to formulate.** (as quoted in Ellis, Richard (2001), Aquagenesis (New York: Viking)"

> "... Science writer Lisa Shawyer concluded: **"Trilobites had "the most sophisticated eye lenses ever produced by nature"** (Shawyer, Lisa J. (1974, "Trilobite Eyes: An Impressive Feat of Early Evolution," Science News, 105:72, Feb. 2)."

Recently some fossils evolutionists have dated even earlier (Precambrian) have been found, but they seem too different to be ancestral to the Cambrian fossils. The oldest and most famous of these are the fossil bacteria dated at 3.55 billion years old which even atheists admit: "look identical to bacteria still on Earth today."[2] Evidence shows:

• Even though modern bacteria are claimed to have gone

[2]Peter D. Ward, Donald Brownlee, *Rare Earth, Why Complex Life is Uncommon in the Universe,* 2000, p. 57.

through 3.55 billion years of being perfected, the oldest fossils look identical to modern bacteria.

• Modern eye lenses are not as good as those first lenses evolutionists date at over 540 million years ago.

Punctuated Equilibrium

In the past, evolutionists generally misrepresented fossil evidence by claiming that the fossils showed a gradual change from one type of plant or animal to another. They mocked or ignored the creationists who said the fossils did not show these gradual transitions because God had created a number of basic categories that brought forth after their kind. More recently, however, two evolutionist scientists also let the cat out of the bag. They, too, insisted that transitional fossils were generally lacking and suggested an evolutionary solution. In doing so, doctors Stephen Gould and Niles Eldredge stirred up an evolutionary earthquake!

> "In 1972, Mr. Gould truly shook up the field when he and Niles Eldredge published a famous paper coining the term "punctuated equilibrium."[3]

Gould explained that slow gradual evolution was contrary to the fossil record:

> "...most paleontologists envisioned new species as arising by the insensibly slow and steady change of entire populations over long stretches of time, ...a notion known as gradualism...
>
> And yet, while thus stating the issue in general

[3]Richard Monastersky, *Chronicle of Higher Education*, 3/15/2002, p. 14.

writings, all paleontologists knew that … the vast majority of species appear fully formed in the fossil record and do not change substantially during the long period of their later existence."[4]

Gould and Eldredge wanted other evolutionists to accept "…the fossil evidence at face value, regarding it as a true representation of how evolution worked"[5] instead of misrepresenting the fossil record to go with the orthodox evolutionist idea of how the fossil record should look. Gould and Eldredge did not think evolutionists should make false claims about the fossil record.

Gould, until his death in 2002, was one of the most anti-creationist evolutionists imaginable, yet it was he who announced that the missing links were really missing and would always be missing because evolution had not occurred gradually as Darwin had insisted. Gould suggested that after long periods without significant change, which he called "stasis," evolution advanced rapidly in small isolated groups of plants and animals. He insisted the groups were so small and the evolution so rapid that they did not leave fossils. The long periods of little change called "stasis" are what the fossils show:

> "Mr. Eldredge and especially the more rebellious Mr. Gould were suddenly telling their colleagues to stand up for themselves and for the message that fossils were sending. "Stasis is data," the two proclaimed."[6]

[4]Stephan Jay Gould, Opus 200, *Natural History*; Aug 91, Vol. 100, Issue 8, pp. 12-16.
[5]Monastersky, *Chronicle of Higher Education*, p. 14.
[6]Ibid., p. 14.

"Stasis is data" means that the stable periods without evolutionary change that the fossils actually show are evidence, and should be studied. Naturally, many evolutionists object to this, and continue to pretend that:

• Transitional fossils are abundant or, on the contrary:

• Gradual transitions happened but the fossils have not yet been found.

One of the best evidences that transitional fossils are lacking is the fact that experts disagree among themselves as to which animals were the ancestors of most groups.

While there was no fossil evidence to back up Gould's solution of rapid evolution among small isolated groups, his idea did point out a way in which evolutionists could honestly admit lack of transitional fossils instead of claiming that fossils showed slow gradual evolution.

Gould did not, however, say there were no transitions at all, and got quite upset when he felt creationists inferred that he did, so I will let him clarify with his own pen:

> "…since we proposed punctuated equilibrium to explain trends, it is infuriating to be quoted again and again by creationists —whether through design or stupidity, I do not know— as admitting that the fossil record includes no transitional forms. Transitional forms are generally lacking at the species level but are abundant between larger groups."[7]

To show how wrong creationists are, he gives two illustrations. One is well known. He calls the Australopithecus afarensis the oldest human. Australopithecus had the head of an ape, the long arms and curved fingers of a tree

[7]Stephen Gould, *Hen's Teeth and Horse's Toes,* 1983, p. 260.

dwelling ape, short legs like an ape, and toes like an ape. The few afarensis fossils that have been found show no evidence of gradually becoming more human like.[8]

In another book, Gould states, "Archaeopteryx, the first bird, is as pretty an intermediate as paleontology could ever hope to find."[9] Archaeopteryx, by a strange coincidence, is the same example those who believe in gradual evolution use to support their position. It was an extinct fossil bird with teeth in its beak and claws on the elbows of its wings. While, for lack of a better example, evolutionists claim it is a transitional fossil between reptiles and birds, it is actually a great illustration of stasis (no change). In his attempt to show a difference between his interpretation of the fossils and that of creationists, Gould gave examples of exceptions he said did show slowly evolving transitions. Did they? You be the judge. Seven or eight fossils of Archaeopteryx have been found, and none were more or less evolved than the others. All are fossils of the same fully formed bird. They show stasis; no evolutionary change from one Archaeopteryx fossil to another.

If either Gould or the gradualists really have fossils showing gradual evolution from one animal to another, why use these examples? People have objected, showing me reports of fossils of dinosaurs they claim were ancestors to archaeopteryx, but evolutionists date archaeopteryx as having lived at the time of the earliest dinosaurs, and the so called "ancestors" as having lived after archaeopteryx.

[8]See Marvin L. Lubenow, *Bones of Contention* for a good discussion of all the fossils evolutionists claim had a part in human evolution.
[9]Stephen Gould, *Bully for Brontosaurus*, 1991, pp. 144-145.

Many evolutionists are backing off and calling such fossils "intermediate" or "intermediary" instead of "transitional." While it may sound like six of one and half a dozen of the other, when a distinction is intended, "transitional" means one evolved from the other while "intermediary" only means that two groups share some characteristics.

The reason the punctuated equilibrium idea "truly shook up the field," was that the thrust of the argument was that the fossil evidence did not show the slow gradual evolution that evolutionists for years had been claiming. Despite the fossil evidence to the contrary, most schoolbooks still promote evolution by insisting that one plant or animal evolved slowly and gradually from another. Some, instead of admitting that evidence for punctuated equilibrium is evidence against slow, steady evolution, now hide the controversy by adding a bit of punctuated evolution to slow evolution. Here is how one schoolbook has it both ways:

> "In many cases, the fossil record confirms that populations of organisms did, indeed, change gradually over time. But there is also evidence that this pattern does not always hold. ...evolution has often proceeded at different rates for different organisms at different times..."[10]

Punctuated equilibrium, however, was not intended as a compromise, but as an ax that would chop off and uproot the dishonest old idea of gradual evolution. Brett wrote:

> "Did life on Earth change steadily and gradually through time? The fossil record emphatically says

[10]K. R. Miller, Joseph Levine, *Prentice Hall Biology*, 2002, p. 439.

'no.' For millions of years, life goes along uneventfully; then suddenly, a series of natural disasters disrupts the status quo... Episodes of rapid evolutionary change punctuate long intervals of stasis, during which little or no change takes place."[11]

Like Gould, Brett is saying the fossil record is emphatically against the claim that living things evolved gradually. It is strange that evolutionists, from the inception of the theory, could firmly believe something which so clearly contradicts the fossil record. In this, Darwin was right. The fossil record does not provide the multiplied billions of transitional fossils that would validate the idea of slow gradual evolution. Brett's quote reminds his fellow evolutionists of what the fossils really show, and tries to get them to quit honoring the traditional evolutionary dogma. The fossil record, rather than evolutionary tradition, should determine what they teach.

The fossil record does not offer evidence for either slow or rapid evolution. Fossils show distinct groups that start fully formed and stay that way until they become extinct. That's more what we would expect if God had created distinct groups of animals. The punctuated equilibrium provides an evolutionary explanation for the lack of transitional fossils, but since it is based on an absence of fossils, it too is unsupported by evidence. My friends who believe in either fast or slow evolution do so by faith! As a creationist, I too have faith.

[11]Carlton E. Brett, "Stasis: Life in the Balance." *Geotimes,* Vol. 40, Mar. 1995, p. 18.

8

Did Life Evolve from Chemicals?

How Did Life Begin?

What an individual believes on this one subject goes far to determine whether he will believe in God or become an atheist. Like it or not, the answers schoolbooks give to this question determine to a large extent, the religion of millions of readers.

Unfortunately, the only possibility most school textbooks consider for the origin of life is natural causes. This is strange because it is contrary to the evidence, and contradicts other pages of the same books. In fact, virtually all biology textbooks say spontaneous generation never happens, that is, living things always come from living things, never from dead chemicals. Here is how one textbook puts it: "new cells always come from existing cells."[1]

This is a statement of one of the most proven scientific

[1]Holt, Rinehart and Winston, *Modern Biology,* 2002, p. 264.

principles, the principle of biogenesis. Biology textbooks explain the experiments and the evidence that led to this conclusion, and clearly state that spontaneous generation does not happen. Scientific evidence, both observational and experimental, upholds the basic scientific principle that new life always comes from existing life.

At this point, a transition is made from statements based on scientific evidence to statements based on atheistic speculation. Most textbooks limit themselves to a naturalistic explanation of how life began, and leave out the possibility that the living God created life. To do that, they make the origin of life an exception to the rule that life only comes from life. They postulate that an imaginary first cell was generated spontaneously. In the case of the book quoted above, after having explained the scientific principle of biogenesis they ask: "How, then, did the first cells originate?" They have just shown scientific evidence that spontaneous generation does not happen, when out of the blue, about one page later, they switch and claim that at one time it did happen. Many books try to cover the fact that they are contradicting themselves by changing the name from "spontaneous generation" to "abiogenesis" which comes from roots which mean: "not biogenesis" which is to say that the first life did not come from something living. The only difference between abiogenesis and spontaneous generation is that abiogenesis is claimed to have happened only once. Their teaching that the first life was an exception to the principle of biogenesis is not based on scientific evidence, but on the atheistic belief system that nature is all that there is.

Generally for something to be scientific, it must be observable and repeatable, but the schoolbooks generally use a different definition of science when dealing with where the first life came from. It is: "The human activity of seeking natural explanations for what we observe in the world around us."[2]

There are two possible ways life could have begun. The evidence points to design and creation by an intelligent God. The other possibility is that life was generated by nature with no intelligent supervision. Defining science so it excludes any solution except the blind forces of nature is a shrewd philosophic solution to the atheist's scientific problem that the evidence favors creation. By switching to this definition of science, most schoolbooks need only consider the "natural alternative" which is against the evidence, against the principle of biogenesis, and against some other laws of science.[3]

Imagine for a moment that you are an atheist. As you step out the front door one morning, there, before your eyes is a brand new Ford parked in your driveway complete with the title and the keys. Where did it come from? The Ford is a product of intelligent design, so, if you use "spontaneous generation by the blind forces of nature" to explain the origin of the Ford, you are going to look foolish. As a result, the definition "science seeks natural explanations" is mostly just applied where it will be an aid to atheism. You can tell the truth about the Ford.

[2]From the Kansas State Guidelines, see Peter Keeting,
"God and Man in OZ," *George*, Oct, 2000, p. 87.
[3]The laws of probability, entropy from the second law
of thermodynamics, and cause and effect.

By defining science in a way that excludes from the science books the evidence that life had an intelligent designer and creator it would seem at first glance to exclude half of the evidence regarding the origin of life. In fact, all the valid scientific evidence is excluded! How can I make such a statement? Let me explain.

I started studying the origin of life with the idea of comparing the scientific evidence that favors an intelligent living Creator with that which favors a spontaneous natural origin. I had read a great deal about the subject, so I began the study believing I would find more scientific evidence favoring an intelligent Creator than abiogenesis. I was also influenced by reading the Bible every day. It explains that God created certain categories of living things. I know the living God, and have found Him trustworthy. This increased my expectation that I would find more evidence supporting an intelligent and capable designer/Creator than abiogenesis.

In spite of all this, I was not prepared for what I found! After reading book after book promoting abiogenesis, from school biology textbooks to books written by expert, origin-of-life researchers, it dawned on me that all I had read were thousands of pages of speculation. Not a single book gave even one shred of scientific evidence that life evolved spontaneously from chemicals. I have had a request out on the widely read www.creationism.org for anyone who has any scientific evidence for abiogenesis to let me know, and no one has. Authors who support the position do it with speculation, scenarios, myths, and made-up stories which they substitute for evidence.

Almost unbelievably, many of the letters I receive from atheists show that they have been completely taken in by the substitution of fables for facts. They don't try to weigh the evidence for and against creation by God to see which seems stronger. They are so used to claims supported by made up stories, that they seem to have actually come to believe that any story, no matter how far fetched it is, trumps any amount of solid scientific evidence to the contrary. Be prepared to resist the temptation to treat speculation as better than evidence.

Most textbooks support their claim of abiogenesis with nothing but a manipulative definition of science and made-up stories. Then they censure out the two kinds of valid scientific evidence:

- That abiogenesis could not and did not get life started.
- That God did in fact create life.

Hiding the evidence for creation to sell students on the atheistic idea of where life came from is so contrary to good science it is one of the top reasons why many thinking people now home school, or send their children to Christian schools.

As you read, prepare to be surprised! I will pile evidence upon evidence; first, convincing and easily understood evidence that life was not produced by natural causes, then evidence for an intelligent planner and Creator.

Were The Materials Available?

You can't make an airplane out of aluminum unless aluminum is available. Reasonable atheists admit that for a first cell to form without a Creator, the materials cells are made of would have to have been available:

"If life indeed started without the help of miracles, the first organisms must have been made of materials that were easily available."[4]

This obvious fact puts textbook authors who oppose the Creator in a terrible bind. As we will see, in spite of many attempts to make students believe otherwise, cells are made of very large molecules that will not form in nature except when assembled by already living cells. The order of their component parts is not determined by chemical bonds, but by the information they are to carry. DNA and RNA are so complex and hard to construct that scientists can't even make them in the lab!

Let's examine a few of the most popular made-up stories about how life might have begun without a Creator. I give them in the order in which they became popular. Notice that, while each of these stories claims that life was started by a different chemical, not one of these chemicals will form in nature except when made by already living cells. The materials that these stories feature were not available!

The Myth That Lipids Formed in Nature and Produced The First Life

If you pour a little oil in water and shake it, the oil separates into little round balls called coacervates which look a bit like some cells. Chemists call oils and fats "lipids." Back when microscopes were too crude to reveal the complexity of cells, some thought these tiny bubbles of fat evolved into cells. Here is a schoolbook explanation:

[4]Iris Fry, *The Emergence of Life on Earth,* 2000, p. 127. See also: Holt, *Biology, Visualizing Life*, 1998, p. 192.

"When mixed with water, certain lipids will form a bubble that is called a coacervate (koh AS uhr vayt) which has a double-layered membrane much like the lipid bilayer of the cell membrane... The early oceans probably contained numerous small lipid coacervates, each one forming and then dispersing. Over millions of years, coacervates that could survive longer by taking in molecules and energy from their surroundings would have become more common than the here-today-gone-tomorrow kind. When a means arose to transfer this ability to "offspring" coacervates, probably through self-replicating RNA, life had begun."[5]

This convincing story is science fiction, and is contrary to the evidence! Both lipids and RNA are too complex to form in nature apart from living cells, so the idea that both formed at the same time, and in the same place with the RNA inside a lipid membrane is also false. Cairns-Smith, one of the most prominent first life researchers, explains that lipids, and the nucleotides which make up RNA, are only formed in the miniature factories of already living cells:

"Though a few organic substances —for instance certain simple amino acids— can form fairly easily under prebiotic conditions, other biochemical building blocks such as nucleotides and lipids, require for their synthesis a 'real factory.' ...The synthesis of these substances involves a series of reactions, each reaction following the previous one in utmost accuracy."[6]

[5]Holt, *Biology, Visualizing Life,* p. 194.
[6]Fry, *The Emergence of Life on Earth*, pp. 126, 176-177; Quoting Cairns-Smith, *Seven Clues to the Origin of Life,* 1985, p. 126.

According to this expert, neither the lipids of cell membranes nor the nucleotides which make up RNA and DNA are produced in nature except by the "real factories" of already living cells. The made-up story we read from the schoolbook quoted earlier, that lipid coacervates with the help of RNA produced the first cell, is not true. But millions read textbooks, and who reads an origin of life researcher like Cairns-Smith? Few if any of the kids and teachers you know will ever discover the truth unless you give them copies of this book.

There was a third false statement in the brief biology textbook quote. Did you catch it?

> "Over millions of years, coacervates that could survive longer by taking in molecules and energy from their surroundings would have become more common than the here-today-gone-tomorrow kind."

Is this true? Does natural selection work on chemicals to eliminate the less fit lipids? No, it only works on things that can keep track of information, reproduce, and pass the information on to their offspring.[7] While lipid coacervates did not exist till living things made them, they have been around ever since living things started producing them, and they are still the "here-today-gone-tomorrow kind."

Though there was no known source for a lipid membrane before real cells were present to make them, lipids would have been vital to a first cell because cell membranes are made of lipids. The first cell had to have a

---

[7]James P. Ferris, "From Building Blocks to the Polymers of Life," in *Life's Origin,* Editor: J W Schopf, 2002, p. 136.

functioning membrane around it, or the other parts would have been so much loose goo dissolving into the ocean.

A cell's membrane, however, must do much more than keep its parts together. If a cell is to live, its membrane must also let in nourishment, expel wastes, and keep out unwanted materials. Lipids can't do all this on their own. A cell with a membrane that did not also contain pumps, channels, and sensors made of proteins would die because it would let water enter but would keep nourishment out.[8]

The Myth That Proteins Formed in Nature and Produced Life

In his famous 1953 experiment, Stanley Miller showed that amino acids could be formed under conditions that might have occurred in nature. Amino acids are the building blocks of proteins, the main ingredients of living things. So a story was made up that claimed that amino acids which had formed in nature then came together to form proteins which then formed living cells. One reason amino acids could not have made proteins is that the amino acids must follow one another in a precise order which is determined by information in the cell's DNA, and is different for each protein. Another is that the natural tendency of amino acids in water is to not link to each other and make proteins. The part of the story about amino acids getting together to make proteins, which then got together to make a cell, was made up by some optimist who wanted to believe that Miller's amino acids had made

[8]Bruce Alberts, etc. *Essential Cell Biology, An Introduction to the Molecular Biology of the Cell,* 1998, p. 347.

the first life. It is contrary to the way chemistry works, but adding it helped Miller's experiment become the most widely publicized origin-of-life experiment of all time.

Before Miller, Oparin had produced "proteinoids," by heating dry amino acids, but they organized into small spheres that will not work in living things. The amino acids in proteins, instead, are hooked together one behind the next like cars in a train, each in a specific order not determined by the chemical tendencies of the amino acids, but by the information in the DNA. The order of its amino acids gives each protein its own specific properties.

Well known origin of life researcher Leslie Orgel contributed a chapter, "The Origin of Biological Information" to the book, *Life's Origin*. Orgel begins:

> "Organic chemists should have invented the computer scientist's motto, 'Garbage in, garbage out.'"[9]

Orgel explains that if chemists have garbage rather than a pure compound going in, garbage will come out. While textbooks use Miller's famous experiment to convince students that chemicals built up to become life, Orgel uses the same experiment to show the extreme difficulty of keeping garbage out of the chemicals which would have been needed for living cells. Orgel writes:

> "For example, Miller's classic experiment …produces tar along with a percent or two of a complex mixture of racemic amino acids …."[10]

[9] Leslie E. Orgel, "The Origin of Biological Information," from the book *Life's Origin*, edited by J. William Schopf, 2002, p. 140.
[10] Ibid.

Orgel is saying three things:

• Miller's experiment, the most famous of all origin of life experiments, produced garbage (the tar) mixed with a percent or two of amino acids which are the building blocks of proteins, the main ingredients of cells.

• The amino acids that made up that percent or two were "Racemic," which means they were a mixture of half right and half left handed amino acids. Proteins will not work in cells unless all their amino acids are left handed. All amino acids produced in nature outside of already living cells are mixed left, and right-handed, and will not work in proteins. Even if there had been a way to produce all left-handed amino acids, they would have had to be used right away, because over time, they break down to half-and-half.[11] Half-and-half won't work, but neither will 90% left handed amino acids, or 99%. Living things require pure left-handed amino acids.[12] The percent or two of amino acids that were produced were nicer garbage, but still garbage because they were racemic rather than all left-handed, and would not work in living cells.

Orgel points these things out to help us understand that unless there is a way that nature can produce all pure left handed amino acids, no useful proteins could have been made. In experiments like Miller's, and in all of nature except in living cells, no pure left handed amino acids, or proteins are formed. In fact, even when scientists buy all pure, left-handed amino acids at a chemical supply house and make a perfect organic broth, no proteins are

[11]See my book *How Life Began*, pp. 15-16, 23-26 for documentation.
[12]Orgel, *Life's Origin,* pp. 73, 151.

produced. Even some schoolbooks now admit:

> "Scientists have not been able to cause amino acids dissolved in water to join together to form proteins. The energy-requiring chemical reactions that join amino acids are reversible and do not occur spontaneously in water. However, most scientists no longer argue that the first proteins assembled spontaneously. Instead, they now tell us that the initial macromolecules were composed of RNA, and that RNA later catalyzed the formation of proteins."[13]

Most of those who rejected their Creator to believe that life started with the spontaneous generation of proteins, have realized that this position was anti-scientific, and have abandoned believing in it for another.

The Myth That The First Living Cell Was Started by RNA

Orgel used his explanation of Miller's famous experiment as an example to point us to the almost infinitely more difficult problem of how the available garbage could have produced the first RNA and then the first cell. He asks:

> "How could chemistry on the primitive Earth proceed in such a messy way, producing information rich living cells, those exquisitely designed chemical factories, from such unpromising starting materials? This is the central and as yet largely unanswered question facing investigators on the origin of life."[14]

[13]Johnson, Raven, *Biology, Principles & Explorations,* 1998, p. 235.
[14]Orgel, *Life's Origin,* p. 140.

Orgel examines attempts that have been made to solve the problem of making RNA out of the garbage that would have been available, but concludes by lamenting that a very large gap separates the huge molecules of RNA from the small molecules of non-living things.[15]

Andrew Knoll, a professor at Harvard, shows that the fact that no RNA was available, nor even the nucleotides from which it is made, makes RNA a doubtful candidate for maker of the first life:

> "Worst of all, even if we could produce the right components, combining them to form nucleotides, the building blocks of nucleic acids, is daunting. To date, no one has figured out how to do it."

Knoll is lamenting that even if a competent scientist had all the right parts to begin with, he could not put them together to make even the nucleotide building blocks of RNA, let alone RNA itself. This information is vital to understanding the origin of life, yet if you search for a public school biology textbook that admits this, you will learn what censorship is all about. Knoll continues:

> "There is still another difficulty. Nucleotides are chiral molecules, which is to say that they come in two forms which are mirror images of each other — like your hands. RNA can be built from right-handed or left-handed molecules, but mixed chains won't grow. How then could RNA —which in cells consists exclusively of right handed nucleotides— have emerged from a fifty-fifty mixture of left- and right-handed building blocks? Again, no one knows.

[15]Ibid., p. 154.

The problems are so difficult that many researchers have given up on the idea that RNA was the primordial molecule of life."[16]

Knoll admits that many researchers are now searching for a simpler substance because they have found no way RNA could have been spontaneously generated even once. However, had there been a simpler substance that worked, and was being perfected by natural selection, it would not have passed the torch to RNA, a different substance that is so difficult to make not even scientists can do it.

While discussing comparative anatomy, evolutionists generally claim that all living things descended from a common ancestor because all have the same basic system of DNA information that controls the life of the cell. They seem not to notice that their claim that the first life came from RNA contradicts their common ancestor claim. The claim that, before life had an RNA-based system, it had a simpler system, makes the contradiction even worse.

Most stick with the made-up story that RNA made the first living cell, claiming it formed on clay, which served as a template on which RNA was built. They cite experiments in which a scientist placed fresh nucleotide building blocks of RNA on clay daily, and some connected to form short strings.[17] When this information filters down to the school book level, it often sounds like clay puts nucleotides together to form real RNA. It does not, and if it did, finding a scientist who would have been able to

[16]Andrew H. Knoll, *Life on a Young Earth*, 2003, p. 79.
[17]*Life's Origin,* James P. Ferris, "From Building Blocks to the Polymers of Life," 2002, p. 123.

place fresh nucleotides on the clay every day before there were any living cells would have been a bit difficult because:

• RNA is so hard to make that intelligent scientists who try really hard can't even arrange chemicals to make its nucleotide building blocks.

• Living cells are the only things in nature that can produce nucleotides.

• If nucleotides did occur, they could not form RNA because all must be right-handed and half of any naturally occurring nucleotides would have been left-handed.[18]

Many textbooks strip out these facts and speculate that RNA did form once from chemicals in nature. Some school textbooks stray so far from the truth as to claim that experiments like that of Stanley Miller produced nucleotides along with the amino acids.[19]

One textbook tells innocent students a much worse whopper: "...RNA molecules can form spontaneously in water..."[20] Why do textbook authors use false statements like these to convince students that life started without a Creator? Surely, they would not falsify evidence if there were real evidence supporting their position.

It saddens me to see atheists use my tax dollars to spread their religion in public school books. It hurts me even more when they spread it by deceiving innocent kids

---

[18]Stanley L. Miller, and Antonio Lazcano, "Formation of the Building Blocks of Life," in the book *Life's Origin*, editor J. W. Schopf, 2002, pp. 98-100.

[19]For example: Holt, *Biology, Visualizing Life,* 1998, p. 192.

[20]Johnson, Raven, *Biology, Principles & Explorations*, p. 230

with false statements. It makes me sadder still that our government permits the establishment of atheism as the religion of our public schools and universities.

Students and their teachers have no idea that there is no evidence to back up the atheistic claims about the origin of life. They trust their textbooks and have no easy way to check up on them. Giving them copies of this book is one of the few ways you and I have to break the stranglehold of atheism on our schools.

To be fair, some textbook authors probably did not know their statements were false. They were convinced by other biology textbooks. After a made-up story finds its way into older biology books, for example the false story that nucleotides form spontaneously,[21] it finds its way into newer books such as Holt, *Biology, Visualizing Life,* 1998, (page 192), which adds another claim, that not just nucleotides, but also RNA would form spontaneously on early earth, (page 193.) If textbook authors feel it is okay to support their position with made-up stories, they should be up front and mention the difficulty their chosen viewpoint has with the evidence from science.

The authors of the book *Rare Earth* believe in abiogenesis and engage in atheistic speculation about life in space, but they do mention the scientific problems with RNA production:

> "Some of the steps leading to the synthesis of DNA and RNA can be duplicated in the laboratory, others cannot. …The problem is that complex molecules such as DNA (and RNA) cannot simply be assembled

[21]*Biology, The Unity and Diversity of Life,* 1989, p. 572.

in a glass jar by combining various chemicals. Such organic molecules also tend to break down when heated…"

"The abiotic synthesis of RNA remains the most enigmatic step in the evolution of the first life, for no one has yet succeeded in creating RNA"[22]

I have looked in vain for such admissions in high school biology books. Even textbooks that avoid obviously untrue statements often slant their presentations to lead students to believe that RNA did form spontaneously from chemicals. Sometimes they do this in ways that first life researchers have found over and over again do not work.

Many adults were first convinced by textbook claims that life started from lipid coacervates. They were later convinced that life came from proteins instead. Now they are even more convinced that it came from RNA. At each stage, they had faith that whatever they were being taught was true science. Their faith, however, was never based on scientific evidence, but on bad science and made up stories. Why wouldn't they believe? The evidence that God created life is consistently censored out of the textbooks, and few find it elsewhere.

A Tough Job for Primitive RNA

After textbooks have told the story that a primitive RNA had formed, they tell what it must have been like. Since no

22Peter D. Ward, Donald Brownlee, *Rare Earth, Why Complex Life is Uncommon in the Universe,* 2000, First quote: p. 63. (See also *The RNA World,* Second Edition, 1999, pp. 68, 159) Second quote: *Rare Earth* p. 65, see also pp. 62-66.

cell existed yet, the imagined primitive RNA is claimed to have performed many of the cell's functions all by itself. We are taught that it self replicated, catalyzed the formation of proteins, and went on to produce DNA. Real RNA is not capable of doing any of these things.

Catalysts speed up chemical reactions. The ability of the cell to catalyze reactions with great efficiency is one of the major reasons cells can make the necessary complex molecules. Their production requires many steps, one after another, in order, very rapidly. The catalytic ability of modern RNA is very limited. Protein catalysts are often millions of times faster,[23] but neither proteins nor modern RNA can produce proteins without the cooperation of a living cell. The claim that primitive RNA could do it alone, is exaggerated. But if RNA could make proteins:

• How could it know to make all the specific proteins needed for the first cell, and only those?

• Why make the hard ones?

• Why would it not just keep making more copies of one easy protein?

There is an even greater problem. If natural selection could work on primitive RNA, and make it successful at catalyzing the formation of the needed chemicals, why would the RNA at that point quit catalyzing these reactions, invent proteins, and turn this job over to them? It wouldn't, and not just because natural selection does not lead things to replace themselves with totally different substances, but also because of the complex ways proteins work.

Each protein will connect and function in only one place

[23] *The RNA World*, Second Edition, 1999, pp. 165-171.

in its cell, so something must get it to that place. Dr. Guenter Blobel received the Nobel prize for discovering the address tags which permit the cell to send each protein to the one place in the cell where it will work.[24]

While a protein is on the way to the only spot where it will function with the proteins around it, it must fold to fit perfectly with the other proteins that will be its neighbors. Unless each protein is properly addressed and folded, it is not only useless, but it will usually cause a genetic disease. IBM has just built the world's most powerful super computer to help scientists find out how cells fold each protein into the unique shape that will let it fit with the surrounding proteins. IBM explains:

> "The scientific community considers protein folding one of the most significant 'grand challenges' —a fundamental problem in science or engineering that has broad economic and scientific impact and whose solution can be advanced only by applying high-performance computing technologies.

> Proteins control all cellular processes in the human body. Comprising strings of amino acids that are joined like links of a chain, a protein folds into a highly complex, three-dimensional shape that determines its function. Any change in shape dramatically alters the function of a protein, and even the slightest change in the folding process can turn a desirable protein into a disease."[25]

[24]Tom A. Rapoport of Harvard Medical School, *Science News,* 10/16/99, Vol. 156, Issue 16, p. 246. See also *Britannica Biography Collection,* Guenter Blobel.
[25]http://www.research.ibm.com/bluegene/press_release.html

The fact that each protein receives information which sends it to the only spot where it can connect and that on the way it folds to fit that spot is powerful evidence. But it is not evidence that a series of lucky accidents happened for each of the cell's many proteins, but that the whole system was set up by an intelligent Creator.

The plot thickens: For a cell to live, it is not enough for its proteins to be sent to the right places and folded correctly on the way, the cell must also maintain the right amount of each protein. This requires an elaborate control system that turns on and off every activity of the cell at the right time.[26] Systems to control proteins would have been of no use until proteins existed, but if RNA could produce proteins before the controls were in place to turn them off, it would have jammed the cell so full of the first protein it started making, that it would have killed the cell.

If proteins were produced by RNA as atheists claim, we should expect:

• Mostly the proteins which were easiest to make.

• Proteins which would not fold properly.

• Proteins without the proper address tags.

• Lethal quantities of any proteins whose production the cell was not yet programmed to turn off at the right moment.

• Proteins (and other chemicals) not useful to that cell.

• Proteins with mixed right and left handed amino acids.

For abiogenesis to be true, a series of events would have to have happened that cannot happen without a designer.

[26]Susan Aldridge, *The Thread of Life, The Story of Genes and Genetic Engineering*, Cambridge University Press, 1996, pp. 47-53.

The evidence not only indicates that life was not begun by chance, but was begun by an intelligent Creator. Perhaps God purposely left these clues for us to uncover.

How Long?

Even atheists have long recognized that the odds against abiogenesis are astronomical. For years, however, they thought enough time was available to reduce the odds against it happening. Almost no informed atheists believe that today! Why?

• Lipids, proteins, DNA, and RNA all break down over time. In addition, proteins, DNA, and RNA gradually switch over to become half right, and half left-handed. Therefore, huge periods of time would not build up large quantities of any of the substances cells are made of, even if they could form in nature.

• Evolutionists say fossil bacteria have been dated at 3.55 billion years ago, not long after they believe earth cooled enough to support life around 3.8 billion years ago.[27]

Many evolutionists believe that after a first cell formed, it must have taken hundreds of millions of years of evolution to produce a bacteria complex enough to leave the oldest fossils. Why? The fossils they have dated as older than any others look identical to some modern bacteria living today.[28] The time left for the formation of the first cell would have been so short that Nobel prize winner de Duve has written:

[27] P. F. Lurquin, *The Origins of Life and the Universe,* 2003, p. 133.
[28] Ward, etc., *Rare Earth*, p. 57. See also *Life's Origin*, p. 173.

> "It is now generally agreed that if life arose spon-
> taneously by natural processes... it must have arisen
> fairly quickly, more in a matter of millennia or centuries,
> perhaps even less, than in millions of years."[29]

If chemicals could come together to form a living cell in
a short time, scientists should be able to make a cell in the
lab. They can't even make its RNA or DNA! They can't
even make the nucleotides RNA and DNA are made of!

Other evolutionists understand the impossibility of life
having formed on earth, and instead claim that life came
here from a planet off in space, but the problems of
evolving life here would all have been present there also.
Space only adds extra problems: the extremely long, cold
trip through lethal radiation in the vacuum of space, and
the hot, violent impact.

If you still believe one of the made-up stories about
lipids, proteins, or RNA having formed the first life
without the help of a Creator, you can put the story into
proper perspective by adding this four word introduction:
"Once upon a time!"

If you believe life arrived on earth from a planet
somewhere in space, three more words must be added to
the introduction: "Once upon a time, far far away!"

Information

The primary purpose of DNA and RNA is to store and
transmit information. In computer terms, we can think of
DNA and RNA as being hardware, while the information

[29]Christian de Duve, "The Beginning of Life on Earth," *American
Scientist,* Vol. 83, Sept.-Oct. 1995, p. 428.

that they contain is software. Both cells and computers have instructions that direct their operation. Where did these instructions come from? And where did the data come from, the information for making and managing each of the cell's proteins, for example.

Atheistic origin-of-life researchers have been hard at work for years trying to find a way that the hardware could have come about naturally. Their studies have instead uncovered more obstacles to the spontaneous generation of RNA or DNA. Judging by their writings, origin-of-life researchers mostly sidestep the software problem. "If we can only show that the hardware had no Creator," some seem to hope, "the software would have written itself." Others favor ideas that the information came from clay, or primordial soup, or sunlight, but how could any of these have contained the information to make a cell? No computer writes its own software. Programmers write it, then we enter our own data. Information comes only from minds, never from matter or energy:

• When archeologists dig up ancient books or inscriptions, they know it did not write itself. Someone wrote it.[30] I know of no scientist who contradicts this, yet even the simplest cells have more information than any ancient book.

• The SETI Institute uses huge radio telescopes to search for extraterrestrial intelligence. Their scientists know that if they find an intelligent message coming from space, it will prove that we are not alone in the universe,

[30]Charles B. Thaxton, "In Pursuit of Intelligent Causes" *Origins & Design,* Summer 2001, pp. 28-29.

but there is other intelligent life out there.[31] The SETI scientists, including the ones who are atheists, count on there being no exceptions to the fact that information always comes from intelligent beings.

DNA does not make proteins, or carry on other day to day activities of the cell; it contains the information that tells the rest of the cell how to do it. When the cell makes a protein, a bit of the information is copied from the DNA to RNA. Since RNA is not quite the same chemically as DNA, the same information is coded a bit differently as it is copied so the information is unchanged. Unless the ability to copy the DNA information in RNA language was available, the first cells that used both DNA and RNA would have died because they could not transmit information correctly. When the RNA arrives with the information necessary to make a protein, left-handed amino acids are lined up in the proper order for that specific protein, and then linked together. Like giving the same message in English, Spanish, and Chinese, the information for making a specific protein is the same when it is carried by DNA, as when it is carried by RNA, and when it is expressed in protein.

None of the steps in transferring the information would have benefitted the cell without the others, so none of them could have been gradually produced through natural selection. All had to be present at the same time for the first cell to function. Atheists believe in unbelievably lucky accidents. I believe in God.

[31] For documentation and further discussion, see my book, *How Life Began*, Chick Publications, pp. 102-103, 131-133.

Atheists believe that cells evolved from chemicals, so they have strong motivation to believe that the first cell was really simple. Hoping to prove their point, they have done research to see how few genes a cell could have gotten by with and still had life: According to Lurquin, "The number is about 300..."[32] Spetner says that if the symbols for the genome of a bacterium were printed in ordinary type, it would fill a 1000 page book[33] Perhaps you want to argue that these estimates are high, that the first cell had less pages. The evolutionist's problem is not how much information, but that no cell could function without some information. Where did it get it?

To make it sound like this is not a problem, evolutionists write me with exotic new definitions of "information" that do not involve this kind of information. Some equate the information in DNA to the tendency of the atoms in minerals to crystallize in one or a few particular patterns. When you study mineralogy, you learn the ways each mineral crystallizes because that is how minerals are identified. Salt does not change its program so it can crystallize like quartz. Unlike crystals, DNA and RNA can carry whatever message. In this they resemble a blank sheet of paper more than a crystal. They can, for example, carry the information for making many different proteins.

The principle dictionary definition of "information" is, "knowledge communicated or received..." The second is "knowledge gained through study..."[34]

[32]P. F. Lurquin, *The Origins of Life and the Universe,* 2003, p. 6.
[33]Lee M. Spetner, *Not by Chance,* 1998, p. 30.
[34]Random House, *Webster's College Dictionary,* 2000, p. 678.

Cells contain and use knowledgeable instructions that work perfectly for making even the cell parts that scientists can't yet make in the lab. When, after years of study, an intelligent scientist decodes the instructions and makes the material of a particular cell part in his own laboratory, will he have shown that no intelligence was necessary? Hardly! He will have added more evidence that a very intelligent creator used real information.

Every cell makes many complex substances that are never put together by chemicals outside of cells. Why? Because its DNA contains the instructions for making these complex substances, and other parts of the cell follow those instructions. Such complex information comes only from minds. God is very smart!

Machines

In every case in which the origin of a machine is known, it was designed by an intelligent designer. This is true of the space shuttle but it is also true of your bicycle.

Cells are full of tiny functioning machines called molecular machines. Their different parts work together to accomplish things that no one part could do by itself. Some of the machines are like tiny but very efficient motors that spin things. Others transport things to other parts of the cell. The ribosomes are tiny machines that link amino acids together to make proteins. To link them, several kinds of proteins work together with RNA following the directions contained in the DNA.

If too much or too little of a protein were made it would kill the cell, so other kinds of machines regulate the process by turning protein production on and off. One of these uses specific stretches of DNA called regulatory DNA sequences. The DNA, however, cannot turn protein production on or off by itself. Each regulatory DNA sequence works with a specific protein that folds perfectly to fit the correct spot on the DNA, and work with it. DNA and protein working together form a machine that regulates the production of a protein. They form a switch that turns a gene for that protein on or off at the right times.[35] Neither the regulatory DNA sequences nor the regulatory proteins can do the job without the other.

To get to the right spot on the DNA, each of the regulatory proteins had to have a fully functioning address tag that would send it to the only spot on the DNA where it would fit and function. On the way, it had to be folded correctly. Otherwise it would not fit when it got there.

Now add this vital evidence: If the machine which makes proteins had been able to make them before the one that regulates them was in place, the runaway production would have killed the cell. The regulator, in turn, is half protein, and would have been useless until its protein existed. The cell could not work until both protein production and the control system were up and running. Many of the cell's other machines are equally essential if the cell is to live. Behe quotes Darwin as saying,

> "If it could be demonstrated that any complex organ existed which could not possibly have been formed by numerous, successive, slight modifications, my theory would absolutely break down."[36]

[35] Alberts, etc., *Essential Cell Biology,* pp. 259-262.
[36] Michael J. Behe, *Darwin's Black Box*, 1996, p. 24.

Behe calls any machine that would not work unless several parts were present and put together properly, "irreducibly complex." Take away any part of a thing that is irreducibly complex, and it won't work. Not only does the cell contain machines which, in themselves, are irreducibly complex, these machines must also work together with other machines of the cell. Now, if one could take away either the machines which make proteins, or the regulatory machines, not one of the cell's other machines which depend on proteins would work either!

In addition, none of these machines could function after the first generation if not for the machines involved in untwisting and dividing the DNA to allow the cell to reproduce. If every other machine in the cell worked, but the cell membrane lacked the protein pumps and channels which allow the cell to take in nutrients, the cell would die and none of its other machines would matter.

With time and research we could add machine after machine to the list of machines which can only work if other machines are working. If an imagined first cell lacked any one of the many essential machines, it would not work. The machines are interdependent. Therefore the machines could not have accumulated gradually. For a first cell to live, a certain number of its machines would have to have been brought on line all together.

Think this through: If just one tiny but essential part of any essential machine was lacking, that machine would not work, and the cell could not live. Compare it to an airplane. Take just one wing off an airplane and it won't fly, but even if it has both wings it won't fly if it lacks the steering mechanism. Here is my point: If all the main components are present, but the steering mechanism lacks just one small but necessary part, the airplane won't work. Just as an airplane designer had to include all the essential parts, so did the cell designer.

We do not know of any complex machine whose parts accumulated gradually with no one directing the process. This is evidence. Those who claim the first cell was an exception honor their presuppositions above the evidence. Schoolbooks that replace scientific evidence with made-up stories are dumbing down students in order to support the world view that there is no Creator.

Why are cells and their machines able to function? Each cell contains in its library of information the directions for making the machines, and the instructions that tell how they are to work together. How did this information get there? Forget the phony theories! How do the directions for making machines get into any database? Does the evidence show that such directions result from a number of lucky accidents undirected by any source of intelligence? No! Never! Such information only comes from intelligent minds.

Even atheists admit that all other machines, from wheelbarrows to washing machines, had intelligent designers. Only in the case of the machines in cells does their commitment to materialism require them to make an exception. Their attitude carries over from the time when they thought cells were simple goo in a sack. Continuing research and better microscopes have revealed one layer of complexity after another. The marvelously coordinated machines of the cell are the worst exception they could make. If atheists claimed that a watch came about by accident we might wonder how they could believe something so contrary to the evidence. But making this claim for cell's machines is even worse than for a watch that automatically resets itself by signals from a satellite. The coordination of the molecular machines is much more complex.

If atheists want to get themselves into such an obvious conflict with reality, I probably should not complain, but why should they drag schoolbooks out onto such thin ice with them? Can't they see that the ice is going to break?

My prayer is that you may understand and act on your newly acquired knowledge to let God bring you into the most wonderful of all relationships. May you know God, and fit with him like a regulatory protein fits the stretch of DNA it was made for.

Conclusion

Many who rejected God thought it was necessary if they were to follow science, but let's face it, many of the arguments used to convince you to believe in evolution were wrong. Haeckel's embryo drawings, for example, have been used in textbooks for more or less the entire 150 years it has been known they were faked. I quoted a number of statements from current schoolbooks that are not true. I also pointed out examples of downhill evolution used to create faith in uphill evolution. If uphill evidence had been available, evolutionists would have used it.

Some attack the Bible when I show them untrue or distorted statements which led them to become atheists.

They claimed the Bible cannot be trusted either. Can it?

The most famous and most commonly used "proof" that the Bible is false says it was impossible for Adam and Eve's sons to have wives and children because the only woman who existed was their mother. While no daughters are named in Genesis chapters three and four, where three sons of Adam and Eve are specifically named, read a few verses farther, and the problem is solved. Genesis 5:4 says that Adam: "...begat sons and daughters." Adam's sons could marry their sisters.

Most cultures don't allow the marriage of close relatives now because their children would inherit the same mutations from both father and mother increasing the risk that the children would be born with genetic diseases. Since these diseases are caused by copying errors in duplicating the DNA during reproduction they accumulate gradually and were not present in the beginning. The Bible is not at fault. Most other points in which the Bible is under attack also have simple explanations.

There is much sound evidence that the Bible is inspired by God, and not simply a human book. For example, it contains many prophecies of specific events still off in the future at the time they were written. Hundreds of years before His birth it was stated that:

• Christ would be a descendent of David (Isaiah 9:6-7, Jeremiah 33:15-16).

    • He would be born in the town of Bethlehem (Micah 5:2).

    • He would die for our sins (Isaiah 53:4-6) with his hands and feet pierced, and that the soldiers would divide up his clothes and gamble for His coat (Psalm 22:16,18).

Check them out! Jesus said, "Believe me that I am in the Father, and the Father in me: or else believe me for the very works' sake" (John 14:11). He was speaking of the miracles those who were listening had seen Him do. But inspiring the Bible writers to include accurate prophecy is another of God's works.

Another is the creation of living things. The solid evidence attesting to His creation leads us to believe in Jesus Christ and in His Father. Belief in Christ is very important because it determines our future:

> "He that believeth on the Son hath everlasting life: and he that believeth not the Son shall not see life; but the wrath of God abideth on him" (John 3:36).

While the Bible promises eternal life to people who trust in Christ, it also offers a way to verify this. It says their lives will be changed in the here and now:

> "Therefore if any man be in Christ, he is a new creature: old things are passed away; behold, all things are become new" (2 Corinthians 5:17).

In fact, we see drunkards and drug addicts leaving their vices and treating their wives and families with love and respect after coming to Christ. The transformation is often very impressive. As a result, most big cities have rescue missions devoted to carrying the gospel to this kind of people. Many thieves have trusted in Christ, stopped stealing, and now work to support themselves and help others.

When I was in college, my roommate lived such an exemplary life, I was not able to brush it off when he explained to me from the Bible that I should trust Christ to save me. The evidence of his life impressed me, but I held my ground, and insisted that I could get to heaven by living a good life. To show him I could, I tried to do it. I made a serious attempt, but it was a dismal failure. I had one particular sin that was an embarrassment to me. I tried to stop, but could not cut it back.

I next convinced myself that my roommate's life was just a result of his unusual personality, not of God working in his life. Eventually I gave in to his invitations and went with him to a youth meeting at his church. There I found a whole youth group like my roommate, and many of them told how God had changed their lives when they trusted in Christ. I was soon convinced that God's work in their lives was real, and before long, I gave in, and trusted Jesus Christ to save me too. From that day my own life was radically changed for the better, just as the Bible said it would be. I watched with amazement as God took away the particular sin I had tried so hard to overcome.

The Bible says,

> "For God so loved the world, that he gave his only begotten Son, that whosoever believeth in him should not perish, but have everlasting life. For God sent not his Son into the world to condemn the world; but that the world through him might be saved. He that believeth on him is not condemned: but he that believeth not is condemned already, because he hath not believed in the name of the only begotten Son of God" (John 3:16-18).

The bad news in this quote is that people who have not trusted Christ are already condemned. Look over your life.

You will see that you too have sinned. Have you trusted the Savior to save you? "He that believeth not is condemned already."

The quote's good news is that God loves you and if you will trust Jesus Christ to save you and give you everlasting life, He will. This is not just an abstract idea. When you trust Christ to save you, God will give you evidence that you are no longer condemned. He will change your life in the here and now. Trust Him to save you and see!

ALSO BY THOMAS HEINZE

**Here is proof
that life could not
have formed in
"Primordial Soup"
billions of years ago,
but required a Creator.**

Evolutionists claim that
simple chemicals became
concentrated in ancient
oceans, forming an organic
broth which eventually
produced living cells.

Heinze reveals the facts evolutionists won't tell you. The
amino acids produced in Stanley Miller's famous 1953
experiment would not work in any living things. The
more recently suggested steps in "chemical evolution"
will not take place either. The idea is scientifically
bankrupt, and the foundation of evolutionary thinking is
destroyed.

Full of quotes from the best known scientists in the field,
How Life Began is a great gift for students, teachers and
school libraries. Learn how the scientific facts speak
powerfully of an intelligent Creator, without whom life
could never have begun. Learn how to know Him
personally. *158 pages, paperback*

ISBN: 978-0-7589-0479-9
Published by Chick Publications

ALSO BY THOMAS HEINZE

ANSWERS TO MY CATHOLIC FRIENDS

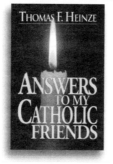

Answers to questions
Catholics frequently ask
Christians. A great help
for sharing the gospel
with Catholics.
62 pages, paperback
ISBN: 978-0-9379-5852-0

ANSWERS TO MY MORMON FRIENDS

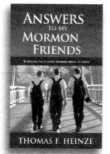

Facts about Mormon
doctrine and Joseph
Smith's life that will help
you witness to Mormons.
80 pages, paperback
ISBN: 978-0-7589-0457-7

ANSWERS TO MY JEHOVAH'S WITNESS FRIENDS

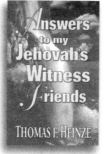

Answers you need to
effectively witness to
Jehovah's Witnesses.
128 pages, paperback
ISBN: 978-0-9379-5858-2

All three books published by Chick Publications.